www.finishinglinepress.com

THEY SAY

poems by

Linda Warren

Finishing Line Press
Georgetown, Kentucky

THEY SAY

ACKNOWLEDGMENTS

The Worcester Review: "Black Ghost"
Diner: "My Brother Calls"
Blueline Magazine: "Stillwater River"
The Mud Chronicles: "Miracle"
Soberistas.com: "Sobriety"

Publisher: Leah Huete de Maines
Editor: Christen Kincaid
Cover Art: Linda Warren
Author Photo: Linda Warren
Cover Design: Elizabeth Maines McCleavy

Order online: www.finishinglinepress.com
also available on amazon.com

Author inquiries and mail orders:
Finishing Line Press
PO Box 1626
Georgetown, Kentucky 40324
USA

Contents

Black Ghost

Kennebago trout will rise
but only to a fly that swims like light.
For years these trout have memorized
the ghost of such a fly, the feathered lure
named for its maker, crack shot, fisherman,
Black Ghost, guide to those who could afford him.

And the wealthy clients' lonely wives,
who could blame them?
They say his moves were graceful, clean
as water flowing through the Steep Bank pool,
they say his hands could call back current
to the gills of fish he'd taken from the stream.
They say that he could slant a woman's thoughts to water.

It may have been, with one, that she was only looking
for something in her life to mark off time,
but there are no markers to the Steep Bank pool.
A railroad bed, untracked, runs through the woods.
You know it only by its history,
swamp-lined in places where the story darkens.

They say she listened to the river,
they say it spoke her language,
they say she trusted it,
they say that its desires were her own.
Beyond this, nothing certain can be known:
they found her husband dead, the lamp
burning, shotgun loaded by the door,
the Black Ghost gone, the pool in flood
along its banks.

The widow told no secrets,
sold the camp, moved on downriver.
The Black Ghost came back home

when the floodwash fell
but would not say where he had been.
No one thought to ask the trout
hovering beneath the steep bank,
remembering how light swims.

Great Blue Heron on the Swift River

I vexed a Great Blue Heron
along the catch-and-release section of this stream
that flows year-round, gift of the accidental wilderness
around the reservoir that quenches Boston.

The heron didn't move far, just to another fallen log,
an easy pebble toss from where I stood.
She looked well fed and feathered,
in this Anthropocene landscape
for which five townships and their homesteads drowned,
and a hundred thousand acres were returned to grace.

She eyed me, fellow wader of this unoccluded water,
then arched her neck and tipped her beak down to the trout
she herself had no plans to release,
a famous beauty deciding which delicacy she desired,
as rich as she needed to be.

Losing the Zonker

It was no place to make a cast:
water too fast to wade and too cold to risk it,
branches overhead, bushes leaning out over the banks,
but the fisherman I met at the bridge swore
there were fish here, in the seam below the big split boulder,
with the whole river roaring through the ravine.

I tied on my favorite Zonker, gold head, royal red
silk thread, strip of rabbit fur and wrap of iridescent green,
amazing fly for fooling fish, all that gleam and wiggle.
Cautious roll casts, checking above, checking behind,
sigh of thanks that I have found a window below the trees.

I hooked a fish, big Rainbow, strong and wild,
pissed off at being foiled by that Zonker, and damned
determined not to be landed no matter how artfully
I used the rod, tip bent over, line taut, and the trout

shook his head, shook out that barbless hook,
which of course snapped back and zapped itself
into a branch too high to reach, too tough to bend.
My last Zonker, *sine qua non* of trout flies, trout conner's daughter,
jewel in the fly box, promised joy of another spring,
embedded in a tree limb high over
that rushing, indomitable water.

Swamp

A hundred acres here that once were woodlot, cart track,
fields, a stream that fed some farmer's pump -

Big Mama Swamp's the landlord now, to beavers
who keep the place according to her stamp.

She's eaten all the trees clean down to bone,
nothing left to break the sky but branch and stump.

She got the wind to take down anything that still had leaves
and underneath the moon she's hung for lamp,

black shadows spike across the snow, like letters
in a language no one speaks—all slash and jagged crimp.

The old foundation by the bank, so many seasons
caulked, graveled, hay-baled to keep out winter's damp

is two feet underwater for all that work,
house, garden, barn, no more than temporary camp.

Big Mama took it for a looking glass
where she, the fairest of them all, could primp.

Calusa Tryptich

> *[The Calusa of Southwest Florida] claimed that each man has*
> *three souls; one is the pupil of the eye, another is the shadow*
> *that each one makes, and another one is the image one sees in*
> *a mirror or in clear water.*
> —*Fr. Juan Rogel, Florida, February, 1567*

1. The Shadow That Each One Makes

I eat breakfast with the fish,
Florida Hilton, Corporate Dining room, aquarium.
I think about work, and you.
The fish think about the business of coral reefs,
small reefs in glass-bound tanks illuminated from the bottom.

You are the angular trapezoidal cruiser, black and white stripes,
wrought iron shadows, mouth in the right place for business.
I'm the blue angel who should be swimming in your wake,
only I'm twelve hundred miles away, and you're glad
    to have me gone.

Years ago, when you led me to the edge of a cliff
looking for eagles, and one of them flew out beneath our feet,
wingspan wider than the space between us,
I thought I would follow you the rest of my life,
into your world of rivers and wood fires,
as if to follow were the only choice.

Watching the fish, I chew some corporate sausage,
contemplate what I'm supposed to know.
You flick your tail and slip into the reef. I tap the glass
    to bring you back.
No dice, you're still in Massachusetts.

I can see you there, looking out at the orchard,
at the slant of light that hasn't changed
since the morning we married, since the night,
years later, counting our salaries, subtracting unpaid bills,

I asked you what we were going to do. You had no plan.
I watched the light come up, then wrote a resume,
three-quarters fiction, and entered that world you so despised.

My blue angel glides out of the tropical colors,
casting her shadow up to the underside of air.

2. The Image in Clear Water

The software is leaking
and for twenty hours we sop it up.
Then Scott, Navjit and I walk into the Florida night
to watch the lightning in the storm clouds over the Gulf.
Near the fountain pond, an alligator.
I ask the all-night guard if that's the infamous Fred.
They're all named Fred, he says.
Another bolt of lightning strikes.
Fish scatter, chasing light.

A Great Blue heron wades out from the shore,
intent on fish, on making a living.
Who knows what obligations drive her,
what invented skills give her bravado,
what mate or young she wades away from?
I lean over, look for my reflection in the water
but I see only glittering ripples from the place where Fred
has slid his long reptilian intentions
into the pond
under the soul of the pulsing sky.

3. The Pupil of the Eye

Black mangroves walk through water slowly
making land. Old reptiles navigate the sluggish current.
Fish undulate below, the crayfish skitter.
I am the only one in a boat.

For passage through this estuary
the Calusa used to levy tolls
and I've paid mine, no argument.
I have a spray can of Florida Swamp Dope
that cost nine dollars at the rental desk
and claims to repel everything that swims or crawls or flies.
I'm afraid to use it on myself;
I don't know which I am.

I wonder if Ponce de Leon knew who he was,
rounding a bend like this to meet
the arrow that stopped his heart,
the black-haired warrior taller than any man
he'd ever seen, hand out for tribute.

I gave at the office, I say out loud
and when I nose around the mangroves,
I meet the Calusa's eyes.
He lowers his bow and spits in the water.
He looks like my husband, an earlier version
I once planned to land my life on.
I'm not sure he speaks my language.

That Spaniard, I say, the one
who came here looking for eternal youth,
I have to admit he never got any older.
He grins. His canoe is better than mine,
as are his attitude, his weapons, and his teeth.

I'm half soaked but it doesn't matter;
the water's warm as blood.
Out in the bay two dolphins
swam by me, one on either side,
came up out of the water to have a look.
I paddled madly, trying to catch them
then had to laugh at myself—

this vestigial urge to follow
what I could never catch.

I start to tell this to the Calusa,
but when I look for him, he's gone.
The word *Abandoned* stabs me
between the second and third ribs,
its aim perfected by repetition.
I stare into the mangroves
where the darkness gathers into substance
and by the time my eyes grow accustomed to the dark,
I notice that my empty boat has drifted down the river,
with my paddles, my binoculars, my Swamp Dope,
that some time soon it will disappear around the island,
toward some destination I thought I intended to reach,
but that for some time now I've been wading,
a solitary woman, finless, wingless, boatless,
in possession of nothing but my own soul,
my eye on the mangroves making their own land.

They Say

Why a silver sea-rich
river fish would rise
to an Oriole-orange Spey fly in September,
when the sun guilds the gold birches
and bronzes the branched oaks,
when the blue of the river
is seven times deeper than the blue of the sky,
and the amber of the tumbled rocks
is brighter than the coat
of the river-edge mink,
and the fire-flame maples
float their offerings
down the current
is a mystery, they say.

Fishing a Wooly Bugger under the Bridge on Potato Head Road

They were hitting on every third cast, that rainy evening.
I must have hooked twenty Brookies, netted and released them,
maybe I hooked some more than once.
They were crazy with lust for that olive green Bugger.
And I was fishing dirty—backcast under the bridge,
forward cast into the honey hole, strip in that abomination of a fly—
chenille and maribou and some flashabou ribbing—
bling and temptation.

A better woman would have tied on a Quill Gordon
or a Hare's Ear nymph, something requiring skill and subtlety
and understanding, philosophical understanding, even,
of the complex interstices of the chain of life.

Me, I went with lust and intemperance.
And those fish and I—we understood each other.

Seeing Through Water

Impossible to believe trout could be invisible in such clear water.
"There must be a dozen," he says.
I peer into the river.
Gin clear, rippling over a fallen tree, a pebbled bottom.
There cannot be anything more.
And yet he seems to see them.
"Lined up along that sunken birch," he says.
I tilt my head, squint, move a step to the side.
There must be something wrong with my eyes.
Or I have fallen out with God,
the vision is given only to those whose faith
floats on the water like a light Cahill;
I have been weighed and found wanting.
"Brookies," he says.
"Liar," I think.
Then a flash of silver, dappled flank, sinuous.
One, two—a dozen, and I can't look away,
afraid to lose this elusive, wavering vision,
this fish-scale grace.

Miracle

The first trout of April shows herself,
a sudden strike and spreading ring
in the glassy water of the cove.

Amazing, how the wind speaks to the water,
ghost-magic, how it paints the water with its passage,
the way the phantom water snake insinuates his sly and supple way
along the edge. The water-skaters appear and disappear.

Starflowers bloom, Hepatica tells profound secrets,
lilies spot themselves like trout,
and over the pool, where I cast my long-tailed feathered artifice
my rod unloads the line according to the laws of physics
and by the grace of graphite and the tapered line,
the fly lights down within the magic center
and the trout rises, takes.

Resplendent splash of lake,
my heartbeat racing to catch the turning world,
and maybe this is not a miracle,
but oh, sweet universe, it's close enough.

Character Study

Coyote is the one
who socializes half an hour, max,
then slinks into the kitchen hall and lurks,
waiting for the house cat.

Coyote waits
like morning seeping underneath a curtain
unremitting, willful, foreordained.

Coyote jewels herself by her intentions:
sequins for seduction, pearls for larceny,
green citrines for secrets,
jade for lies.

Coyote speaks four languages:
the body's passions, recollection,
blood in all its moods, scents in the dark.

Coyote sleeps by day,
at night she carries heat beneath her skin.
The darkness fits her like a sleeve.

Coyote holds no mercy in her eyes.
To meet her gaze is grave; you will know
the name she calls the moon,
and ever after when she howls
you'll hear her hunger.

Casting Practice

Under a blue Equinox sky,
on the soccer field behind the school
he props the rod case in the snow,
strings up with a hundred feet of six weight line.
A good rod, graphite, not bamboo,
But built on the memory of bamboo.
The arc of the backcast lifts the line,
Again, again, until his muscles
recollect the skill,
the forward snap that shoots the line
straight out over the snow on this field,
where there is no water
and there are no salmon.

The backcast, the perfect flick
of hand and arm, again, again,
leaves marks in the snow,
set side by side precisely,
as if there were a current to drift
them invisible.

This is not his river
but the memory of his river
flows in him like water
flowed through gills
of the hookbill salmon
after the hook was freed,
and the fish held facing the fast water,
the relentless tug of current,
the fierce resistance
that directs him home.

My Brother Calls

My brother calls. It's late. He's drunk. Not much has changed. The FBI still trying to kill him. His boss and his coworkers, bribed to lie. He wants retribution for the girl he loved, who was raped and murdered by men she didn't know. He will not forget. Her name was Dierdre. Her hair was brown and fell across her shoulders like the trailing feathers of an angel's wing. They shot her in the head. It's not your fault, I say, that's not your fault but he doesn't hear me, and I can't stop the tide of words that pulses through the phone I grip white-knuckled, trying to sort out the truth.

I sit at the top of the cellar stairs and stare at grey concrete, thinking of a grey and amber river, imagining the current pulling at my feet, the rod bending to the flick of my wrist—arch, return—the line launched across the air to settle where the ripples meet the pool. The tug—and then the reel sings, "Here, Here!" in the fine voice of milled machinery, the will of the fish runs through the line, but the fragile tension holds, and everything about it is absolutely true.

He'll sue, my brother says. He'll sue the bastards, and he'll win. Fifty million he'll get, and the FBI headquarters building—he'll rename it. I think of San Francisco, fifteen years ago, eating abalone, watching the kites fly over San Francisco Bay, blue water, Alcatraz in the distance. The San Andreas fault is overrated, my brother said, and made me laugh. Where are you? I say now, and the hangs up on me. I call him back; listen to the phone ring.

I bring the phone with me to bed. Some nights I dream that I am with him, in a beach house. We are young, and close; we share the stonework of belief the house is built on. But it is raining, and the tide comes in, over the porch, running though the house until we stand up to our knees in the current, reading the rapids, noting the deep places: There, my brother calls, and we both stare into the water, looking for a single glint of silver.

Wanderer

Wanderer, why don't you write to me
from the fog-bound islands, the passionate sea?
I saw you standing on the shore
strewn with broken glass, staring.

"I've made a study of it," I think you said,
but remembered words are slippery
like eels, and just as hard to kill.
I'm older now than you ever got before you left,
and no wiser, maybe not even as wise as either of us was then.

I recollect a morning when we rowed out on the bay
in the wooden skiff you built in the cellar
where you hid the whiskey bottles
behind the long pans where you soaked the gunwales
to be fitted, sanded, painted.
We pulled flounder after flounder
into that seaworthy boat and rowed it home.

Tying a Sow Bug on a #16 Nymph Hook

There's that damn mylar strip, supposed to imitate
the carapace along the back. Slippery stuff;
like trying to lash down a good intention.
But you load it up with thread and crowd the eye,
the fly's no good at all with all that scruff.

This sow's a bottom bug, you have to weight it,
lead wire, tungsten bead—you wouldn't think
it would take so much. The average day
is full of things that sink: boots in the mud, hopes,
someone you love who won't put down a drink.

The hook shank's dubbed with seal's fur
tiny hank plucked out and twisted on,
just enough to spiral down the length.
Worse than wasteful, what we thought was needed:
advice that should have been held back, that chance now gone.

A trick of balance, what's necessary, and no more.
To keep your mouth shut, to stand back from the open door.

Pantoum for My Brother's Dog

The dog stretched out beside me was my brother's.
He said she was the sweetest dog he knew.
The dog with her great head resting on my shoulder
was once my brother's dog—now mine, yet—his.

The sweetest dog he knew, and one he loved
as he could love a dog, without restraint,
as once my brother's love was mine, mine his
the two of us against a treacherous world.

You can love a dog without restraint,
an unwrapped gift, with no entanglements.
Dog and gun against a threatening world,
no sister asking, *Please. Don't do this. Please.*

Unwrapped, unnerved, I dream in tanglements,
in fishing lines, in veins to the heart exposed,
no one's sister now. No point in asking.
What's left behind is something undefined.

Love is the heart with open veins exposed,
the dog with her great head resting on my shoulder.
What's left behind is something undefined:
the dog stretched out beside me was my brother's.

Dead Mouse in the Liquor Cabinet

Caught in the snap trap, dead as a mouse in a snap trap,
next to the Scotch bottle.

What did he want with the liquor cabinet?
All I ever wanted was the buzz, and for that
I wouldn't be deterred by a dead mouse.
Close my eyes, reach for bottle, twist off the cap.

The mouse still there, in fact, through three replenished drinks.
Each one, easier to ignore him,
portent of doom as he was, poor sap.

Still, he tripped a few passing thoughts.
Just cruising by, on the way to the crackers?
Living dangerously, brain-wracked,
seduced by peanut butter,
caution to the winds—you can do it, in and out,
but then that whap.

Living to a ripe old age
is a hope we presumably shared,
making our way through the maze.
And now I guess I'm left alone to carry on.
Me, amidst these bottles,
and no map.

Sobriety

I saw a slant of light that dazzled me.
Hard to tell where it came from,
looking against the sun
filtered through trees.

Still, I would have climbed it, drunk with delight,
to be transformed by glamour
and spellcast into someone else.

But there was something of the truth
that held me back, that made me look instead
at the gravel riverbed under my boots
to look for a long time,
and finally to see through the clear water
the sinuous, graceful shapes
of silver trout in the current.

Stillwater River

In the deep hole along the far bank
trout hold in clear water.
I cast a tiny nymph and let it sink down to the stream bed.

My line straightens at the end of the drift,
swings into the current below me.
There's pleasure in watching the way
the line lies across the water,
the way the fly is knotted to the delicate tippet.

It is a good day to be sober.
It is a good day to remake a life.

To tie a Perfection knot, you make a loop,
then a second, in front of the first,
and lay the loose end of the line between the two.
You reach through the first to grasp the second
and pull tight. The original loop becomes
the knot around what's left.

This knot once fastened will not slip.

The Seals of Lubek

Rain talking to the water,
curtain whisk of wind.

The harbor seals come swimming in
sleek and wet, rising, diving,
tidal sweep and harbor bells,
sea streaming from their flanks,
the seals glistening with joy.

Catalogue of Sins with Commentary

I have poached a trout from the river on the day after the season closed. I ate the evidence, which was delicious.

I have spent $65 on a Wursthof oyster knife, ordered online after drinking several glasses of wine. The sin of gluttony comes to mind, but I'm going with alcohol-induced recklessness.

I have left my husband because his heart was incomprehensible to me, and returned to him months later after learning of his cancer coming back, because I didn't have the heart, incomprehensible to me, to abandon him. One of these acts was a sin.

I have checked my Yahoo account during work hours. I have read the Washington Post during work hours. I have ordered jewelry supplies online during work hours. I have accepted a salary bonus offered to me by my boss.

I have listened to innumerable hours of Public Radio fundraising without calling in a pledge.
I have committed the sin of despair, waking from a dream of someone's daughter stillborn, me weeping inconsolably, unable to protect my children from mortality, or pain, or me.

In 1964 I stole a Library book: Leonard Lee Rue's Guide to the Birds of North America, which I still consult from time to time.

I have had my doubts about the character of God. Given the circumstances of life, this doesn't strike me as a sin, but God may dispute this.

I have not asked for forgiveness, yet I have stood deep in a river, casting my line into the current, watching my fly swing downstream, again, and again, while the river raveled itself around me and the wind laughed, and the sun increased by exquisite measures on the water, and I have not cared whether I caught a fish, and my sins have lifted from me, like ephemeral river mist.

Watching Caddis on the Miramichi

I want
> not to be so

human.
> I want so much

more; less.
> I want to be

hatched to what I become,
> to feel my skin

stretch, split,
> my wings, unfolding

to air,
> to the terror

of want,
> of transformation.

Tips on Fly Fishing for Salmon

Don't hook yourself on a backcast.
Don't hook your guide, either.
Don't hook a rock, which will snap off the fly,
    and you will never find it again,
no matter how much you look in the place
    where you know it was snapped off.

If you don't want an audience watching you cast,
    bring your dog with you;
she will provide a distraction.
Don't hook the dog.

Try not to catch your boot on a submerged rock while hollering at
the dog, and fall into the river.
If you fall into the river, try to make it be in July.
Try to make it be not in a fast current.
Try not to curse at the slippery rocks, or the treacherous current.
If you feel inclined to pray, pray for the river. You might as well back
a winner.

There will be a span of time when you are casting into the current
and the sun is setting behind you
and the surface of the river turns to molten gold.
Memorize this.
If you are inclined to pray, pray for memory.

When you flub a cast, and the fly lands ten feet in front of you
in a tangle of line, leader, and hook,
do not curse the line, the wind, the rod or the luck of the caster.

Cursing is acceptable, however, when you lose a fish formerly
    attached to your hook.
particularly when the fish is the largest salmon you have hooked
    all week,
and shakes off the hook after one spectacular jump.
When your guide says, wisely, that you can't land them all,

try not to whine that you didn't want to land all of them,
   only THIS one.
If you are inclined to pray, consider postponing
until you are in a more reverent state of mind.

Forgive the dog for wandering off while you were cursing.
Forgive yourself for losing track of her.

If a beaver disturbs the river with rude beaver-tail slaps over
   holding salmon,
stop casting. Do not hook the beaver, which, if hooked,
will swim off with your hook, your line and probably your rod.
Do not let the dog dive into the pool to chase the beaver,
which, if provoked, may swim off with your dog.
Do not dive into the pool yourself to chase the beaver.

If you hook a salmon and manage to keep it hooked
through leaps, and runs, and headshakes and swirls,
and you bring it to the net,
and grasp it in front of the strong and muscular tail,
to slip the hook from its jaw,
aim the fish upriver, and release it,
and it darts away from you,
bless it on the rest of its journey upriver to spawn.

When the full moon rises over the river,
shining a shattered reflection on the restless water,
watch it rise.

Linda Warren has worked as a teacher, writing instructor, Romance novelist and software analyst. She has published a dozen novels and had poems published in in *The Worcester Review, Diner, Whiskey Island Magazine, Naugatuck River Review, Writing the Land,* and other books and journals. She has been nominated for a Pushcart, and is a past winner of the Frank O'Hara prize for the poem, "Black Ghost." She fishes the trout and salmon rivers of New England and New Brunswick as often as she can, and this collection is inspired by those rivers and the hours she has spent standing in them, casting for fish and for words.

www.ingramcontent.com/pod-product-compliance
Lightning Source LLC
Chambersburg PA
CBHW022100080426
42734CB00009B/1433